5/92

DOMESTIC WASTE

© Aladdin Books Ltd 1992

Designed and produced by
Aladdin Books Ltd
28 Percy Street
London W1P 9FF

*First published in
Great Britain in 1992 by*
Franklin Watts Ltd
96 Leonard Street
London EC2A 4RH

ISBN 0 7496 0743 2

A CIP catalogue record for this
book is available from the
British Library.

Printed in Belgium

The publishers would like to
acknowledge that the
photographs reproduced within
this book have been posed by
models or have been obtained
from photographic agencies.

Design	David West Children's Book Design
Designers	Flick Killerby Steve Woosnam-Savage
Editor	Elise Bradbury
Picture research	Emma Krikler
Illustrator	Ian Moores

The author, Dr Tony Hare, is a
writer, ecologist and TV
presenter. He works with several
environmental organisations,
including the London Wildlife
Trust, the British Association of
Nature Conservationists, and
Plantlife, of which he is Chairman
of the Board.

The consultants: Jo Gordon is
the team leader of Waste Watch, the
national agency for promoting
recycling in the United Kingdom.

Jacky Karas works for Friends of
the Earth and operates as an
independent environmental
consultant. Prior to this she was
a Senior Research Associate at the
Climatic Research Unit at the
University of East Anglia.

SAVE OUR EARTH

DOMESTIC WASTE

TONY HARE

GLOUCESTER PRESS

London · New York · Toronto · Sydney

CONTENTS

INTRODUCTION

When we bundle up our newspapers, food scraps and other rubbish and leave it to be collected, we rid our homes of waste. However, it does not just disappear when we throw it away. Most rubbish is buried at huge sites, where it can take decades to rot away.

Waste is also piped away from our sinks, baths and toilets. This does not simply vanish either. It has to be expensively treated to make it safe.

The amount of waste from our homes (called domestic waste) is tiny compared to the amount produced by factories and farms. Nonetheless, we are running out of locations to dump the ever-increasing quantities we throw out. Rubbish, sewage and litter are not only a smelly annoyance, they can also be deadly. Waste sometimes contains dangerous substances and can even spread diseases.

We cannot live without creating some waste. However, we can minimise the amount we produce, and put the rest to work for us. Most rubbish can be re-used, recycled or burned to provide energy. Whatever is recycled today saves resources for the future. Recycling also prevents used goods from becoming waste and polluting the environment.

◄ **Many of the things we do at home, from gardening to making dinner, creates waste. Rubbish tips spring up near every town and city to deal with this waste. At the Fresh Kills site near New York City, the piles of rubbish are growing to the size of large buildings. This is a needless waste; many of the things we throw away can be used again or recycled into new products.**

WHAT A WASTE

Every year the world produces more household waste than the year before. This is partly because the world's population is growing. But the industrialised countries, which have relatively low population growth, generate the greatest amounts of waste. The United States alone produces 19 per cent of the world's rubbish.

The main reason for this is that people in industrialised countries have more money, so they buy more and have more to throw away. This trend has been encouraged by advertising, which suggests that people should buy new goods and get rid of their old ones.

Many modern products are purposely designed so that they do not last long. They are made for cheapness or convenience, and have to be regularly replaced. The worst excesses of our throwaway society are goods made to be disposed of after one use, like disposable cameras and razors, and plastic cutlery. These are a waste of resources and also create a lot of rubbish.

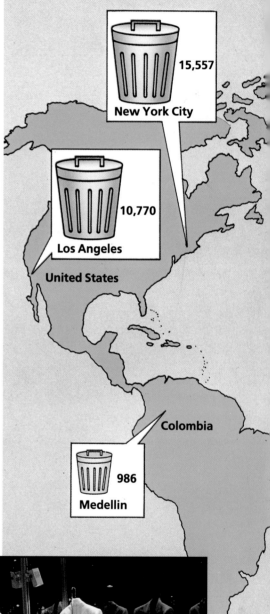

▲ ▶ In poor countries, people collect re-usable items from rubbish. Wealthy lifestyles are more wasteful. For example, as fashions change, clothes are discarded before they wear out.

WASTE (IN TONNES) THROWN OUT EACH DAY IN SELECTED CITIES

Daily waste

Cities vary in the amount of domestic waste they produce. Wealthier countries throw away more. Calcutta, in India, has a larger population than London, but generates less than half as much waste. New York City is the world's biggest producer of rubbish.

KEY

Large barrel = over 5,000 tonnes
Med. barrel = 1–5,000 tonnes
Small barrel = under 1,000 tonnes

AROUND THE HOME

Most of our daily activities produce some sort of waste. We bring our shopping home in carrier bags which are then thrown away. Preparing food leaves behind food scraps and packaging, like tins, bottles, and plastic wrappings. Newspapers, magazines and junk mail are also put in the bin nearly every day.

We often throw out dangerous substances with the rubbish. Paint tins and other containers are thrown out with some of their original poisonous contents still in them. In our gardens, grass cuttings and fallen leaves pile up and must be disposed of. Each time we wash the dishes or have a bath, dirty waste water is left over. Even heating our homes and cooking our food on gas stoves creates waste in the form of gases.

All the waste produced around the home ends up outside it: in tips, in sewers, in the ground, even in the street as litter. With the millions of homes around the world creating more rubbish every day, waste has become a serious concern.

Bathroom
Dirty water from baths and toilets, empty shampoo bottles, toilet roll and soap packaging are all waste from bathrooms.

Garage
Old tins of paint, bottles of white spirits, insecticides and other poisonous household products are thrown out with the rest of the rubbish.

Garden
Grass clippings, fallen leaves, pet waste and other garden rubbish all need to be disposed of.

What's in the bin?
Every day, each person in the United States throws away 1.8 kilograms of waste. Seventy per cent of this is paper, food and garden waste. These will slowly rot down. An increasing amount of plastic is also thrown away, which decays extremely slowly. In cities, where tonnes of rubbish are generated, it increases much faster than it rots away.

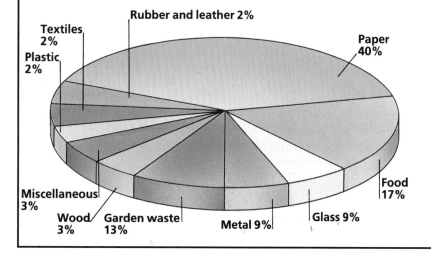

Rubber and leather 2%
Textiles 2%
Plastic 2%
Paper 40%
Miscellaneous 3%
Wood 3%
Garden waste 13%
Metal 9%
Glass 9%
Food 17%

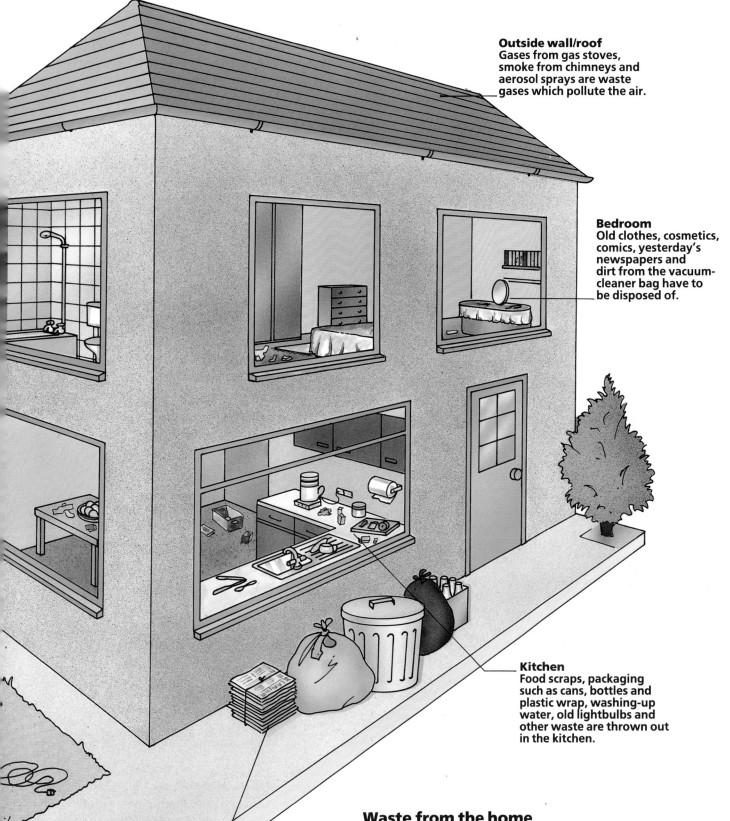

Outside wall/roof
Gases from gas stoves, smoke from chimneys and aerosol sprays are waste gases which pollute the air.

Bedroom
Old clothes, cosmetics, comics, yesterday's newspapers and dirt from the vacuum-cleaner bag have to be disposed of.

Kitchen
Food scraps, packaging such as cans, bottles and plastic wrap, washing-up water, old lightbulbs and other waste are thrown out in the kitchen.

Rubbish can be separated into cans, glass and paper, and much of it recycled.

Waste from the home
An average European home fills 100 dustbins' worth of rubbish a year. One estimate suggests that a British person generates about 10 times their own weight in household rubbish in a year: that means 100 bottles and jars, two trees' worth of paper, 70 food cans, 90 drinks' cans and 45 kg of plastics.

DIRTY WATER

Each time we flush the toilet or pull the plug from a bath or sink, water carrying detergents, bleach and dirt drains into the sewers. In industrialised countries, this waste water is often treated at sewage plants to clean it before it is released to the environment. However, sewage plants cannot always deal with the chemicals we pour down our drains. These may remain in the water when it enters rivers or the sea, and can poison wildlife.

More problems are caused when sewage plants cannot treat the huge quantities of dirty water produced. When this happens, sewage can be released directly to oceans. The sewage contains nutrients that cause small plants called algae to grow rapidly, forming a thick layer on the water's surface. This is called eutrophication.

When these algal blooms die off, their process of decay uses up oxygen, suffocating the other living things in the water. Algal blooms have occurred off the coast of Japan, in the Mediterranean and the North Sea, resulting in the deaths of large numbers of fish.

▶ **Sewage treatment plants now operate in most industrialised areas. They work by speeding up the process of natural decay, making the remaining waste easier and safer to dispose of. The left-over water is purified and can then be re-used.**

A SEWAGE TREATMENT WORKS

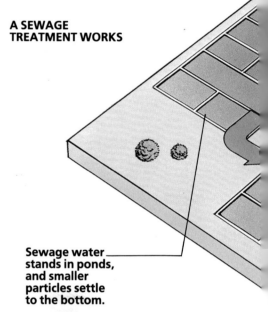

Sewage water stands in ponds, and smaller particles settle to the bottom.

◀ **Dirty water is the world's greatest killer. Every year about five million children die from dysentery, a severe form of diarrhoea, which can be contracted from drinking water contaminated by sewage. In poor countries, like Ghana (shown here), open sewers run in the streets, and people are in constant danger of catching diseases from the filthy water. Clean water can be provided if sewage plants are built, but these are very costly.**

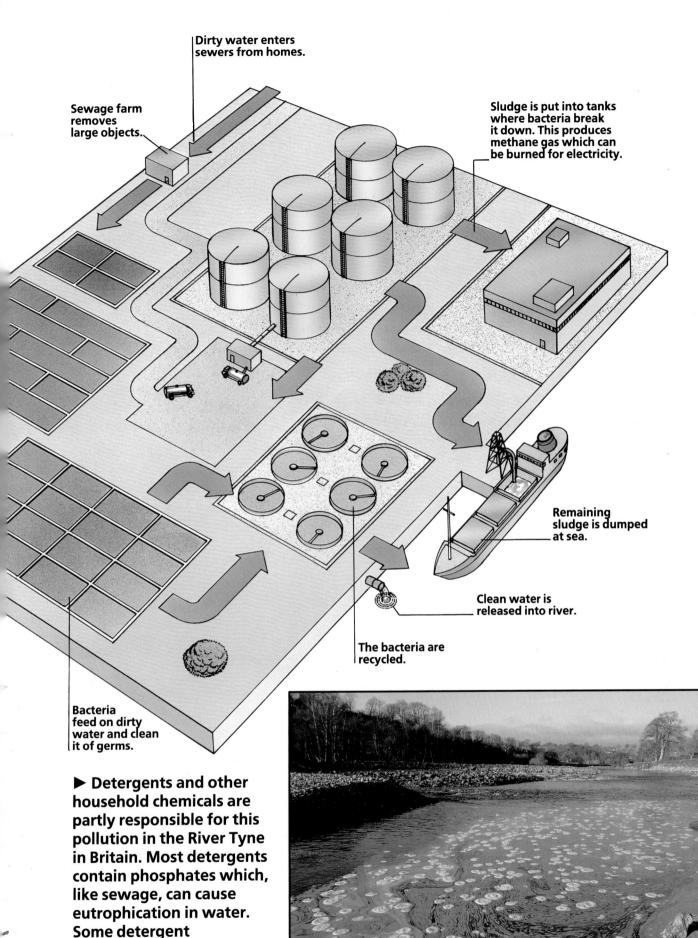

Dirty water enters sewers from homes.

Sewage farm removes large objects.

Sludge is put into tanks where bacteria break it down. This produces methane gas which can be burned for electricity.

Remaining sludge is dumped at sea.

Clean water is released into river.

The bacteria are recycled.

Bacteria feed on dirty water and clean it of germs.

► Detergents and other household chemicals are partly responsible for this pollution in the River Tyne in Britain. Most detergents contain phosphates which, like sewage, can cause eutrophication in water. Some detergent manufacturers have now removed phosphates from their products.

HOUSEHOLD POISONS

Some products which are useful around the home are dangerous to living things when they are disposed of. Bleach is a very effective cleaner. However, when it drains down into the sewers with waste water it kills the bacteria that break down sewage at the sewage plant.

Common household batteries contain poisonous heavy metals. These are believed to cause cancer and other diseases. When dangerous wastes like these are thrown away with the rest of the rubbish, precautions cannot be taken to ensure they do not leak into the environment where they can harm living things.

There are alternatives to many household poisons. Bleach that breaks down naturally can now be bought. Other poisons can be recycled; old frying oil ("chip fat") can be made into fuel oil which can be used for heating.

▼ **Many dangerous wastes are used around the home and then dumped in with the rubbish. Empty containers of white spirit, typists' correction fluid, motor oil, toilet cleaner, antifreeze, rat poison and even disposable cigarette lighters still contain small quantities of poisons. If these chemicals leak into the rest of the rubbish, they make it poisonous. Then when it is buried, rain can wash these dangerous substances into the ground or into water supplies.**

◄ If dangerous wastes are collected separately they can be disposed of safely. In Britain, the city of Sheffield has a specially designed vehicle which visits homes, schools, hospitals and factories to collect dangerous wastes. The vehicle is sometimes known as a "toxic taxi". The poisonous wastes are then carefully disposed of in special sites (left). Some cities in Japan, Germany and the United States also have schemes to collect poisonous waste from homes separately from ordinary rubbish.

► There are 550 million cars in the world. Each one requires the oil in its engine to be changed when it gets too dirty. Although it is illegal in many countries, when a car's oil is changed at home, the used oil is often poured down storm drains or into the ground. Car owners in the United States pour 42 million litres of waste oil into the ground every 10 days. This is the same amount the *Exxon Valdez* oil tanker spilled off the coast of Alaska in 1989, causing major environmental damage. Oil is very poisonous – it only takes a tiny amount to pollute soil and water. In addition, oil which has been in use in a car engine picks up various harmful substances, like heavy metals, which can cause cancer.

WASTE GASES

We produce waste around our homes that we cannot even see. When we spray aerosols, smoke cigarettes, light a barbecue or use air fresheners, gases are carried away into the air. Some of these gases contribute to life-threatening kinds of air pollution.

Inside the house, smoke from cigarettes is believed to cause lung cancer. Fumes given off by solvents (substances which dissolve things) found in paint thinners and glue can also be threatening to health.

Air pollution is not just bad for your health in an immediate sense. Some of these gases are a long-term danger. Burning gas, coal or wood in boilers, barbecues and bonfires releases a cocktail of gases, including carbon dioxide, a gas that helps to trap heat in the atmosphere, keeping the Earth at a temperature suitable for life. This natural phenomenon is called the Greenhouse Effect. However, the huge amount of carbon dioxide we release from industries, cars and homes could be heating up the planet too much. This "global warming" could affect the climate, possibly causing flooding in some places and droughts in others.

▼ Gases can escape from all sorts of ordinary household goods. Chemicals called CFCs (chlorofluorocarbons) are used in some aerosol cans to propel the liquid out. CFCs are released when these cans are sprayed. CFCs are also used in fridges to keep them cool. When the fridges are scrapped, the CFCs escape. They slowly rise to the layer of ozone in the Earth's atmosphere, where they release chlorine which destroys ozone. The ozone layer is essential to life because it shields the Earth from harmful radiation from the Sun. Recently governments have become aware of the dangers posed by CFCs, and are now acting to phase them out.

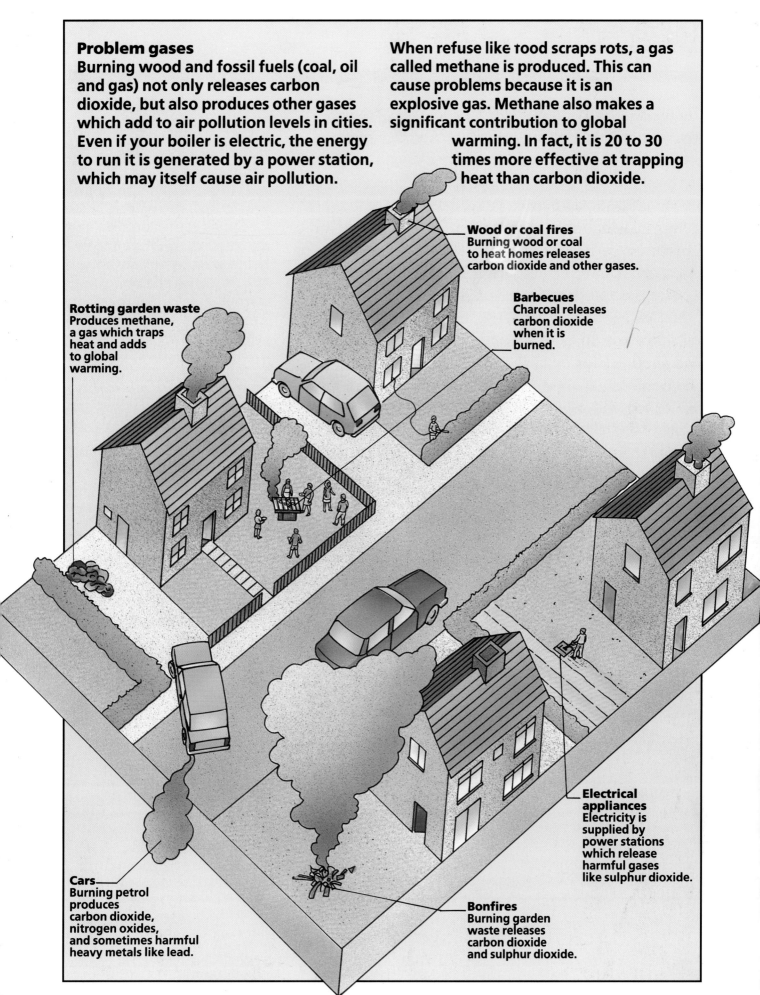

Problem gases
Burning wood and fossil fuels (coal, oil and gas) not only releases carbon dioxide, but also produces other gases which add to air pollution levels in cities. Even if your boiler is electric, the energy to run it is generated by a power station, which may itself cause air pollution.

When refuse like food scraps rots, a gas called methane is produced. This can cause problems because it is an explosive gas. Methane also makes a significant contribution to global warming. In fact, it is 20 to 30 times more effective at trapping heat than carbon dioxide.

Wood or coal fires
Burning wood or coal to heat homes releases carbon dioxide and other gases.

Barbecues
Charcoal releases carbon dioxide when it is burned.

Rotting garden waste
Produces methane, a gas which traps heat and adds to global warming.

Electrical appliances
Electricity is supplied by power stations which release harmful gases like sulphur dioxide.

Cars
Burning petrol produces carbon dioxide, nitrogen oxides, and sometimes harmful heavy metals like lead.

Bonfires
Burning garden waste releases carbon dioxide and sulphur dioxide.

BURY IT?

The vast majority of the world's rubbish is taken to landfill sites. When it arrives it is packed down tightly and covered with soil to stop it from blowing away and to cover the stench. North America and most European countries dispose of more than 70 per cent of their domestic waste in landfill sites.

Although landfills are a relatively cheap and easy way to dispose of waste, they are not problem-free. Lorries pour into landfill sites non-stop, dumping waste much more quickly than it can decay. Eventually sites become full and close down. It becomes increasingly difficult to find enough sites for all the waste. In 1978, the United States had 20,000 landfills; today there are less than 6,000. This is partly because the price of land is rising, making landfill sites more expensive. Public pressure also affects the option of burying waste – no one wants to live near a rubbish dump.

▼ **One of the concerns about landfills is their potential for causing ground and water pollution. When it rains on waste tips, the water becomes contaminated as it drains through the rubbish. If the water seeps into the soil, it carries the pollutants with it, eventually reaching groundwater (the water which supplies rivers and wells). Groundwater pollution threatens wildlife and drinking water supplies. Even modern landfills which are lined with plastic can leak if their lining ages and decays.**

HOW BURIED WASTE POLLUTES SOIL AND WATER SUPPLIES

Rain washes substances from the soil covering the rubbish.

Water seeps through buried waste, picking up harmful substances.

Ground-water carries pollutants to wells, rivers and other water supplies.

Waste to energy

Landfills contain such huge quantities of waste that an enormous amount of methane gas can be generated as the rubbish decays. If the gas is not controlled it can cause an explosion. Methane can also start fires at waste tips. But methane from landfill sites can be put to good use. At very modern sites, like this one near Los Angeles, the methane is collected in pipes, which run to a plant where the gas is burned to generate energy. This site sells the energy it makes to a regional electricity supplier to pay its running costs. At present, it provides electricity for 100,000 people.

◄ The original idea behind landfills was that rubbish could be regularly taken away from homes and put where it would eventually break down. Oxygen, sunlight and bacteria aid the process of decay. But such large quantities of rubbish are packed into landfill sites that sunlight cannot get through and the bacteria cannot do their job. Certain plastics can take 500 years to decay. A newspaper that was found in a landfill was still readable after 30 years.

Well

Pollutants can end up in the environment where they can harm wildlife. Also, they are absorbed by the soil and can affect plants.

River or sea

BURN IT?

An alternative to burying domestic waste is to burn it at very high temperatures in an incinerator. Burning can reduce the amount of waste by up to 90 per cent. Japan and Sweden burn half of their household wastes and Denmark burns 75 per cent, using the heat produced to generate electricity for local towns.

However, burning does not entirely solve the problem of domestic waste. The ash that is left after incineration has to be disposed of, and it can contain dangerous pollutants. For example, burning cannot destroy the heavy metals in batteries. There is also a risk that gases released from incinerators can carry pollutants. Dioxins, chemicals which have been linked with cancer, can be produced when plastics are burned.

Because of these dangers, in most places incinerators are now required to remove toxic particles from the gas before it is released. These controls make incinerators expensive to run. Their high cost can help to encourage recycling, because in places where there are few landfill sites, recycling is cheaper than building expensive incineration plants.

▼ Researchers are looking into ways to use rubbish as an energy source. Some programmes are operating which compress refuse into pellets which can then be burned as fuel. A Belgian scientist has invented a machine that compacts kitchen waste under great heat to get refined oil (below). If this process could be repeated on a large scale, the oil produced could be used to supplement limited oil resources. However, burning rubbish still wastes resources that could be recovered by recycling.

HOW INCINERATION WORKS

Sorting rubbish
At some incinerators, when the rubbish arrives at the plant it is sorted before incineration to separate out materials that will not burn. This includes metals, glass and sometimes plastics. These are either taken to landfill sites, or preferably they can be collected for recycling.

Gases
The gases generated during burning can carry harmful substances. Modern incinerators clean, or "scrub", the gas very efficiently before it leaves the plant. However, high levels of dangerous chemicals have been reported near some incineration sites, although it cannot be proved that they have been released from incinerators.

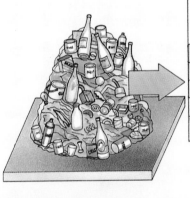

Supplying electricity
The heat created by incineration is used by some plants to generate electricity. The incinerator or the local community can use this energy, saving coal, oil and gas resources. If the electricity is sold, it can help to pay the high cost of operating an incinerator. But not all incinerators are designed to use this energy source.

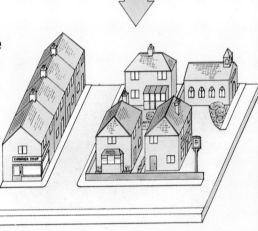

Ash
Incineration creates ash – one tonne for every 4-5 tonnes of waste burned. This is usually taken to landfill sites after being treated to remove any toxic substances. Sometimes ash from incinerators is made into breeze blocks or other building materials. Liquids used to clean the gases also need to be disposed of.

RECYCLE IT?

Once materials become waste, the best way to lessen the problems they cause is to recycle them. This reduces the rapid increase of waste, and is also a source of new goods. Recycling is not a new idea. People have been salvaging the useful materials from their rubbish for centuries. The trade in metal from old pipes and cars, old roof slates and discarded clothes has been set up for some time. Many things can be used again in their original form or they can be made into new goods.

Recycling has many advantages. It often takes less energy to make goods from recycled materials than to make them from scratch. It saves resources that would otherwise be used to make new products. It can also save money, because the cost of disposal is avoided.

For all its benefits, recycling is still not common practice. In some places it is inconvenient, and can be expensive if waste has to be transported long distances to recycling centres. Yet the number of recycling schemes around the world is increasing. Japan now recycles 40 per cent of all of its waste.

▼ Fast-food containers are one of the most wasteful forms of packaging. The food only spends minutes in the containers before they are discarded. Now the polystyrene used in fast-food cutlery, burger boxes and coffee cups can be recycled. This solves several problems. Polystyrene and other plastics take hundreds of years to break down naturally. If they are thrown away as waste they become a long-lasting problem in the environment. Recycling plastics prevents them from becoming litter and saves the resources they are made from.

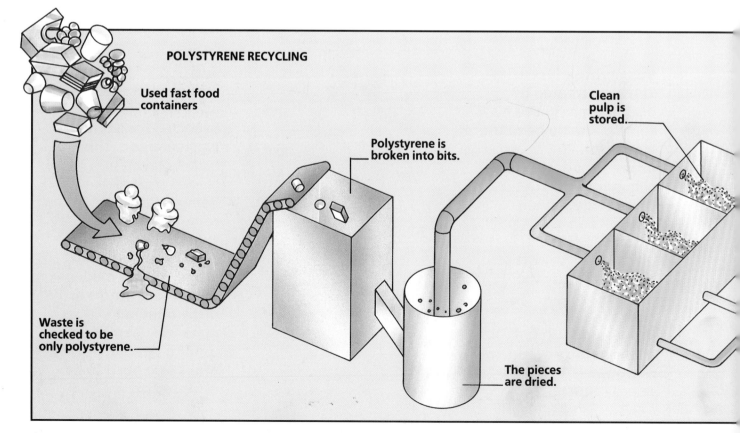

POLYSTYRENE RECYCLING

Used fast food containers

Waste is checked to be only polystyrene.

Polystyrene is broken into bits.

The pieces are dried.

Clean pulp is stored.

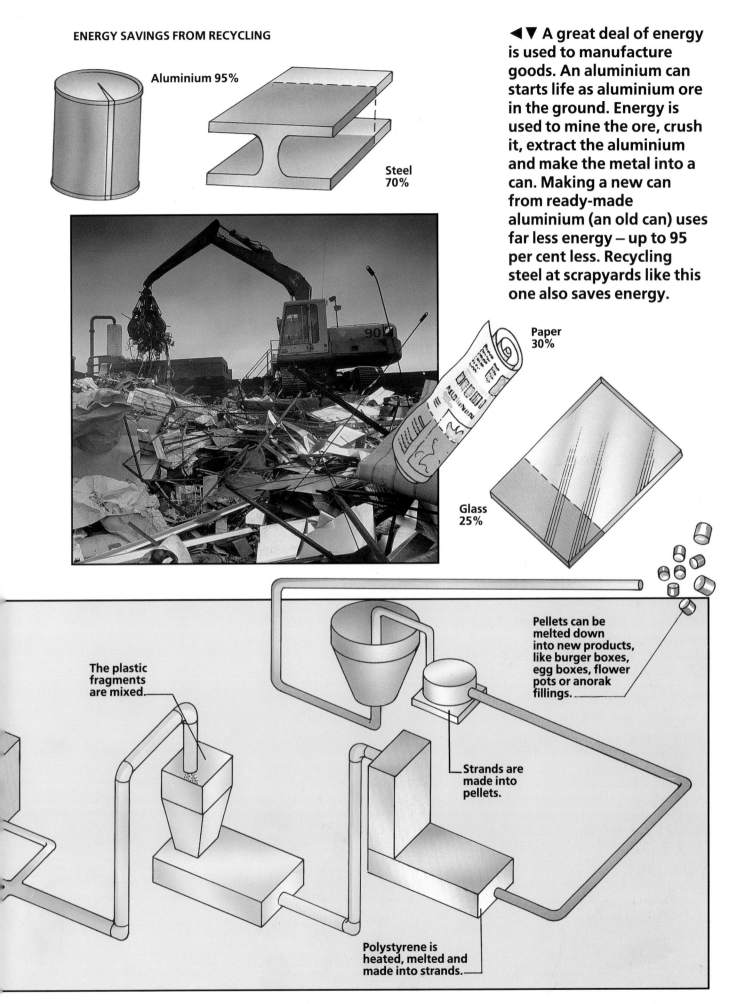

ENERGY SAVINGS FROM RECYCLING

Aluminium 95%

Steel 70%

◄▼ A great deal of energy is used to manufacture goods. An aluminium can starts life as aluminium ore in the ground. Energy is used to mine the ore, crush it, extract the aluminium and make the metal into a can. Making a new can from ready-made aluminium (an old can) uses far less energy – up to 95 per cent less. Recycling steel at scrapyards like this one also saves energy.

Paper 30%

Glass 25%

Pellets can be melted down into new products, like burger boxes, egg boxes, flower pots or anorak fillings.

The plastic fragments are mixed.

Strands are made into pellets.

Polystyrene is heated, melted and made into strands.

RUBBISH AS A RESOURCE

At least 60 per cent of domestic waste can be recycled or re-used. Over a third of what we throw away is paper. Whole forests are planted to meet the demand for paper, which is just wasted although it is easy to recycle.

Most countries are making an effort to make recycling easier for people. One of the problems with recycling is that it involves the time-consuming practice of sorting what is re-usable from what is not. The town of Hesse, like others in Germany, deals with this by separately collecting paper, glass, metal, some plastics, medicines, batteries and some food and garden waste.

The British government has set a target of recycling about 25 per cent of all domestic waste by the year 2000. The city of Portland in the United States currently recycles over 25 per cent, and aims to recycle up to 52 per cent. What is not recycled is dumped in landfill sites where methane gas is burned to generate electricity.

▼ **Many people heap their kitchen scraps and pet waste in the garden, where they rot and make good fertiliser for plants. This is called composting. These Turkish villagers have another way to re-use dung from their animals. They dry it into bricks that can be burned for fuel.**

▼ **There is a long way to go before we are recycling as much as we can. In the United States, the largest producer of waste, only 11 per cent of total household waste is recycled.**

US HOUSEHOLD WASTE

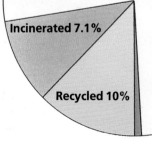

Deposited in landfills 82%

Incinerated 7.1%

Recycled 10%

Composted 1%

Look for the signs

All over the world, countries are recycling more of their waste. This recycling yard is in Budapest, Hungary. You can easily recognise recycling locations by the three arrow symbol, which is widely used. Recycling facilities are user-friendly. Bottle banks are designed to prevent broken glass from flying out when bottles are thrown in. A glass bank is provided for each colour of glass.

◀ Some communities in the United States use "reverse" vending machines (left) to encourage people to recycle. These refund money for glass, metals and plastic.

▼ Clothes can be given away to be re-used, or they can be recycled. Used clothes are collected at this Italian plant. The fabrics are shredded and made into new clothes or blankets.

WHAT CAN BE DONE?

The best solution to the problem of waste is to avoid producing it in the first place. We can go a long way towards achieving this by making small changes in our lives. We can buy goods thoughtfully, choosing loose fruit and vegetables, for instance, rather than pre-packed ones which create unnecessary packaging waste. We cannot always avoid creating waste, but buying re-usable or recyclable products is one way to cut down the amount we produce.

Public concern about waste has led to legislation which encourages recycling. Starting in April 1992, shops in Germany will have to recycle or re-use all packaging returned to them by customers. We need to look at all the ways we can reduce household rubbish. Recycling should be seen as an investment for the future.

▼ Resource recovery systems are very efficient schemes for dealing with waste. They burn household rubbish to heat a local area, and recycle whatever is left. This block of flats dumps its waste down a chute, where glass and metals are separated out and recycled. The rest is burned to heat other buildings. Over 700 resource recovery systems are in use around the world, including a large one at Disney World in Florida.

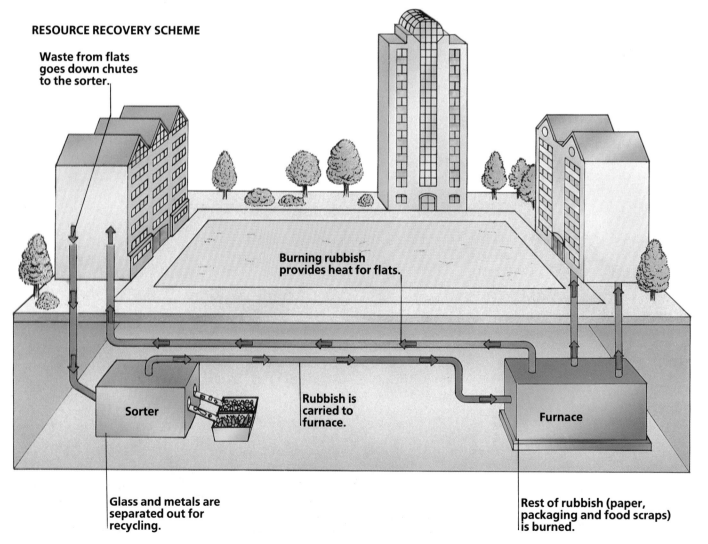

RESOURCE RECOVERY SCHEME

Waste from flats goes down chutes to the sorter.

Burning rubbish provides heat for flats.

Sorter

Rubbish is carried to furnace.

Furnace

Glass and metals are separated out for recycling.

Rest of rubbish (paper, packaging and food scraps) is burned.

▲ Car manufacturers are working towards making their vehicles totally recyclable. BMW claims that its new Series 3 cars are 84 per cent recyclable. The green tint shows recyclable plastics, and the blue the recycled plastics in a new BMW. The metal from the car body and the glass from the windows can be recycled. Seat material can be shredded to make soundproofing for new cars, and engines and gearboxes can be restored to top working condition and used again. Car recycling centres, where all old cars can be taken for recycling, may become familiar in the future. Volkswagen in Germany have started such schemes already.

▲ Re-using household products is the best way to decrease the amount of domestic waste. Returnable bottles can be washed, refilled and used many times. Milk bottles are used on average over 20 times. Carrier bags can be used until they wear out, and clothes and other household items can be taken to jumble sales, car boot sales (above) or charity shops.

In the natural world, everything is recycled and nothing is wasted. When a plant or animal dies it is broken down and consumed by other living things. In this way life forms return to the soil, where their nutrients are taken in by plants. Nature's recycling methods can be used to cut down our waste, too. Scientists in Germany are researching how micro-organisms could break down abandoned Trabant cars, which have been discarded by their former East German owners in favour of Western models. Trabants are made of resin and cotton wool waste. If these micro-organisms prove successful in breaking them down, bacteria could be used to dispose of other items as well.

WHAT YOU CAN DO

You can help to reduce the world's growing piles of waste:
- Buy products with the least packaging.
- Re-use things instead of throwing them out.
- Recycle anything you can – glass, cans, paper and plastics. Contact an environmental organisation to find out what recycling services are available in your area.
- Take any usable waste you have to charity shops or jumble sales so someone else can use them.
- Ask your council to send someone to your school to talk about what is being done about waste in your area.

Useful addresses:

Friends of the Earth
26-28 Underwood Street
LONDON N1 7JQ
Tel: 071-490 1555

Friends of the Earth has written a regional recycling guide with the *Daily Telegraph* which includes a wealth of local contact addresses.

Waste Watch
68 Grafton Way
London W1P 5LE
Tel: 071-383 3320

Waste Watch provides information on all aspects of recycling domestic waste. They have a free pack available for use in primary schools.

Designing a poster:

One of the most important things you can do is to make more people aware of the problems caused by domestic waste. One way you can do this is to make a poster to hang up at school.

1) Think up a striking or clever heading for the poster which will grab the attention of people passing by.

2) Design an illustration or symbol like the one shown here, or cut pictures out of magazines and make a montage that conveys the main message.

3) Read through this book and try to summarise in about 30-40 words what domestic waste is and why it is a problem that affects everyone.

4) Again by reading through the book, make some suggestions as to how we can reduce the amount of waste we produce.

5) Include some other information if there is room, such as useful addresses to contact for more information about recycling, and suggestions of your own on dealing with our growing piles of rubbish.

FACT FILE 1

Disappearing resources

Most of the products that we use at home every day are made from materials, like metals, known as finite resources. This means that there is only a limited amount of them and supplies will eventually run out. The resources which provide the energy for manufacturing, like coal (right), are also running low. Recycling is necessary to conserve these supplies for the future. Estimates vary on how long the Earth's resources will last. There may be enough of some metals to last several more centuries. But scientists are less hopeful about our energy reserves, especially oil.

Domestic waste sometimes contains items made from tropical timber, such as discarded wooden ornaments or pieces of plywood. Although wood is a renewable resource (because trees can be replanted), forests are being cleared for timber far more quickly than they can grow back.

WASTEFUL WORLD

THE AMOUNT OF RUBBISH WE PRODUCE INCREASES EACH YEAR. UNSIGHTLY DUMPS ARE GROWING UP AROUND THE WORLD'S CITIES. WE ARE RUNNING OUT OF ROOM FOR ALL THIS WASTE. AND WE ARE RUNNING OUT OF RESOURCES TO MAKE THE GOODS WE WASTEFULLY THROW AWAY.

WHAT CAN YOU DO?
- RECYCLE AS MUCH AS YOU CAN. PAPER, METAL, GLASS AND EVEN PLASTICS CAN OFTEN BE RECYCLED.
- RE-USE PRODUCTS WHEN YOU CAN — THIS SAVES RESOURCES AND CUTS DOWN ON WASTE.
- AVOID EXTRA PACKAGING.

USEFUL ADDRESSES

The waste trade

As landfill sites near major cities fill up, waste has to transported to sites further away. Some household waste travels hundreds of kilometres to its final resting place. Waste is usually transported by barge or train to its eventual destination. This is a very costly process. Nonetheless, with the cost of landfill and incineration rising, some countries have found it cheaper to ship domestic waste to faraway locations, or even abroad, to dispose of it. In 1989, an American waste disposal firm closed a deal to ship thousands of tonnes of household waste to a Pacific atoll in the Marshall Islands.

Methane digester

Sewage can be a useful resource. Organic waste from homes and livestock can be put into a methane digester, where bacteria break it down, producing methane. In China and India, small tanks provide enough methane to burn for a family's cooking and heating. In the Netherlands and Belgium, large biogas plants produce electricity for whole areas.

Walking waste disposers

China's third largest city, Tianjin, produces 5,000 tonnes of rubbish every day. Tianjin has found a cheap and effective way to dispose of this waste. Pigs eat all the edible refuse, and their manure is collected for fertiliser. Research is being done to use cows as waste disposers. They will eat newsprint, and if soybean printing ink is used, cows can be fed on old newspapers.

FACT FILE 2

Excess packaging

The amount of packaging around some products is unnecessary. A box of chocolates may have up to seven layers of packaging: silver foil, the plastic trays, cardboard, the box that the chocolates come in, the plastic film around it, the paper bag the chocolates were put in when they were bought, and the gift wrapping. Some packaging is necessary to keep food fresh and safe from contamination. But often packaging is used because manufacturers are trying to present goods more attractively or to make the product look bigger. Manufacturers then increase the price of the product to cover the costs of all the packaging. An estimated 10 per cent of the average family's weekly shopping bill in developed countries is spent on packaging, most of which is simply thrown away. If consumers refuse to buy goods that are over-packaged, manufacturers will be forced to get rid of unnecessary packaging.

Record on recycling

Different countries vary in the amount of domestic waste they recycle. Poor countries may not be able to afford modern recycling technology, but people there are more conscious of not wasting anything. Countries everywhere are increasing the amount of waste they recycle in response to public pressure and the realisation that it can save money and resources. Paper is a good example. In 1980, Switzerland recycled 35 per cent of its paper; by 1988 the figure had risen to 61 per cent. Tunisia doubled its recycling to 8 per cent between 1984 and 1988; Sri Lanka increased from 9 to 22 per cent in the same period; and Britain and the United States stayed fairly constant, recycling around 10 per cent of their waste paper (below).

GLOSSARY

Biogas – the mixture of carbon dioxide and methane given off by rotting food scraps and other waste. This gas can be collected and burned to provide energy.

CFCs (chlorofluorocarbons) – extremely long-lasting gases which are used in some aerosol cans and to keep fridges cool. When they get into the atmosphere they damage the ozone layer, which is vital to life. CFCs are now being phased out.

Domestic waste – waste that comes from people's homes.

Eutrophication – the increase in nutrients caused when pollution, such as sewage or detergents, enters the water. This can cause massive growths of algae, called algae blooms.

Global warming – the gradual increase in the planet's temperature, caused by the increasing amount of carbon dioxide in the atmosphere produced by burning fossil fuels. If it changes the Earth's climate drastically, global warming could have disastrous effects.

Greenhouse Effect – the natural warming effect of the Earth's atmosphere. Some gases, such as carbon dioxide, called greenhouse gases, allow energy from the Sun to pass through the atmosphere to warm the Earth's surface, and then trap the heat that rises back into the air. This keeps the atmosphere and the planet warm. It is known as the Greenhouse Effect, and is one factor in making life possible on Earth.

Recycling – processing waste to make it into a form where it can be used again. All sorts of waste can be recycled, such as cans, paper, glass, oil and kitchen waste. Usually waste is taken to a particular place for recycling – glass goes to a glass recycling factory, for example, while kitchen waste can be put on a compost heap.

Solvent – a substance which can dissolve other materials. Water is an example of a solvent. Nail polish remover is another example; it dissolves nail polish. When some chemical solvents get into the environment they can be harmful to people's health.

Waste – something which is considered to be no longer useful. Anything from empty drinks cans to industrial chemicals to washing-up water can be waste. Most wastes can become useful resources if they are recycled or re-used.

INDEX

Photographic Credits:
Cover, page 12, 13 bottom and 30: Roger Vlitos; pages 4-5, 6 right and 28 top: Spectrum Colour Library; pages 6 left, 14 and 29 top: Robert Harding Picture Library; pages 10 and 22: The Hutchison Library; pages 11 and 21: Science Photo Library; page 13 top: The South Yorkshire Hazardous Waste Unit; pages 17 top and bottom, 18, 23 bottom left and bottom right and 25 bottom right: Frank Spooner Pictures; pages 23 top, 25 bottom left and 28 bottom: Eye Ubiquitous; page 25 top: BMW Motors; page 29 bottom: The J. Allan Cash Photo Library.